Bob W...
WA...
FOR ALL SEASONS

Published by Gazette Media Company Limited, Gazette Buildings, Borough Road, Middlesbrough TS1 3AZ. Tel 01642 245401. Fax: 01642 210565. Printed by Juniper Publishing, Juniper House, 3, Sandy Lane, Melling, Liverpool L31 IEJ

ISBN 0-9528814-6-2   © Gazette Media Company Limited, 2001.

Contents

Foreword		5
About the author		6

SPRING

Walk 1	Grosmont & Beck Hole	8
Walk 2	Hinderwell & Staithes	11
Walk 3	Loftus, Hummersea & Upton	15
Walk 4	Sadberge Circular	18
Walk 5	Stanghow & Moorsholm	21
Walk 6	Wensley & Bolton Hall	25

SUMMER

Walk 1	Clay Bank & Greenhow Plantation	30
Walk 2	Cringle Moor Circular	33
Walk 3	Easington & Roxby	37
Walk 4	Lastingham & Hutton le Hole	41
Walk 5	Littlebeck & Falling Foss	44
Walk 6	Old Byland & Tylas Farm	48

AUTUMN

Walk 1	Castleton Circular	52
Walk 2	Great Ayton & Holmes Bridge	55
Walk 3	Hett Circular	59
Walk 4	Lealholm South	63
Walk 5	Sunderland Bridge & Croxdale	66
Walk 6	Wass Circular	69

WINTER

Walk 1	Carlton Miniott & Sandhutton	74
Walk 2	Maltby Circular	78
Walk 3	Nunthorpe Station & Ormesby	81
Walk 4	Redcar & Marske	85
Walk 5	Richmond & Skeeby	88
Walk 6	Stokesley & Broughton Bridge	92

WALKS FOR ALL SEASONS

Foreword

Dedicated to all my walking companions past and present.

WALKING is one of the great joys of life, isn't it? There's no great outlay on equipment but there are endless amounts of pleasure in terms of enjoying our superb landscapes at first hand - with plant, bird and animal life all around.

And, of course, it's good for our health too!

In many ways it makes sense to tailor walking activities to the time of year and prevailing weather conditions with shorter, level routes in the winter months and longer, demanding journeys in summertime and these considerations have influenced this latest selection of walks.

Most of the routes are clearly waymarked along well-defined paths, making it easier to follow the Country Code as we savour the delights of varied landscapes during the changing seasons of the year.

- Bob Woodhouse

About the author

BOB Woodhouse has been writing, broadcasting and lecturing on aspects of local history for the past 30 years.

An early interest in the countryside and the rich history of the North-east was fostered by Alan Falconer, who wrote the Rambler column in the Evening Gazette for many years and was also the author's history teacher at Acklam Hall Grammar School in Middlesbrough.

Bob has literally followed in his mentor's footsteps by becoming a regular contributor to the columns of the Evening Gazette over a period spanning two decades.

After spending almost 30 years in teaching, he retired from full-time work in December 1994 in order to pursue research and writing projects.

He now lives in Middlesbrough and is currently working on several aspects of North-east history as well as on a novel set in Cleveland during the early nineteenth century.

The countryside wakes up

SPRING time is many people's favourite season. Lighter days offer the chance to venture a little further afield and take a closer look at the awakening countryside.

Many of the year's earliest flowers - including the lesser celandine - are yellow, but the most endearing image must be the glorious swathes of snowdrops. Other common flowers include the primrose and wood anenome.

Early spring sees butterflies such as the peacock emerging from hibernation in barns or sheds and the handsome marsh marigold adds a splash of colour to water meadows.

Walks in this section range from dramatic coastal scenery near Staithes and Hummersea to delightful woodland areas in East Cleveland and the Esk Valley to the rolling countryside close to Darlington and in Wensleydale.

Warm, waterproof clothing and stout footwear remain of prime importance and great care is needed along coastal sections where cliff tops are unstable.

Seasonal mists and fast-failing daylight when conditions are cloudy and overcast are other factors to bear in mind and, although these walks cover fairly short distances, it is important to allow plenty of time to complete a safe return during daylight hours.

WALKS FOR ALL SEASONS — **SPRING: Walk 1**

Grosmont and Beck Hole

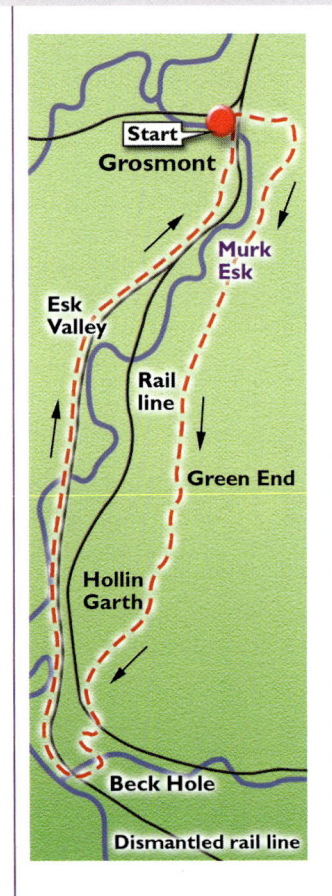

NORTH YORK MOORS

Making tracks deep in the valley

START: Grosmont Railway Station.

DISTANCE: 5 miles.

GOING: Some gradients and muddy sections in woodland on outward half. Return stretch is along level former rail track.

REFRESHMENTS: Venues in Grosmont and Beck Hole.

MAP: Ordnance Survey Outdoor Leisure 27 North York Moors Eastern Area.

WALKS FOR ALL SEASONS — SPRING: Walk 1

THE North York Moors Railway runs through delightful countryside between Grosmont and Goathland but footpaths offer the chance to savour the valley of the Murk Esk at even closer quarters.

Starting from Grosmont station, we head eastwards up the hill and just before the red-brick Park Villa turn to the right (away from the roadway) through a wicket gate. The path runs downhill to a step through stile and over two becks to join a trackway. As we turn left along the track you may spot some Jacob's sheep in the field opposite before heading up the slope.

Before the metal gate we turn right into the woodland and the path soon bends to link up with a stone trod. The well used route climbs through woodland before levelling out and then sloping downhill to a wooden footbridge. Continuing ahead through Crag Cliff Wood, we cross the beck and follow the bottom edge of the woodland to a stile on the right (with a dog flap).

The River Esk at Grosmont

After crossing another small beck, there's another dog-friendly stile and after continuing ahead for a short stretch, the pathway veers to the right to cross a footbridge.

We then make our way up the slope to a field gate where we bear left to rejoin the trod as it runs between hedgerows towards farm buildings at Green End.

WALKS FOR ALL SEASONS   **SPRING: Walk 1**

Passing between posts, we continue ahead through a field gate and then turn left for 100 yards up a trackway before heading to the right on the bridleway that runs between farm buildings.

There are more stiles before we reach Hollin Garth Road and turn right to follow the roadway round to the left and then over the railway track before dropping down into the pretty hamlet of Beck Hole.

At the White House, we leave the public road and pass through a field gate to follow the track beside the beck towards another gate. Turning right along the line of the old rail track, we soon spot a stone (with plaque) which marks the site of Beck Hole Station.

The level gravelled surface makes for easy walking after the woodland sectors on the outward section and you may well see highland cattle and rare breeds of sheep in fields on the right of the track. Continuing along the rail track, we make our way down a step and along duckboards before turning left on a stony track that runs through woods and down another flight of steps to a bridge.

Our route then heads along a gravel track before passing over a footbridge and through to the red brick old school building and nearby cottages.

The track runs ahead to a metal gate and we then turn left through a kissing gate to follow a stony pathway up the slope to a flight of steps and gate.

There are two more gates before we turn to the right down a slope and at the next set of gates we head left through a kissing gate along the Rail Trail to pass the church (on the right).

A suspension bridge carries the final section of the walk over the Murk Esk as we head back to our starting point at the railway station.

WALKS FOR ALL SEASONS **SPRING: Walk 2**

Hinderwell and Staithes

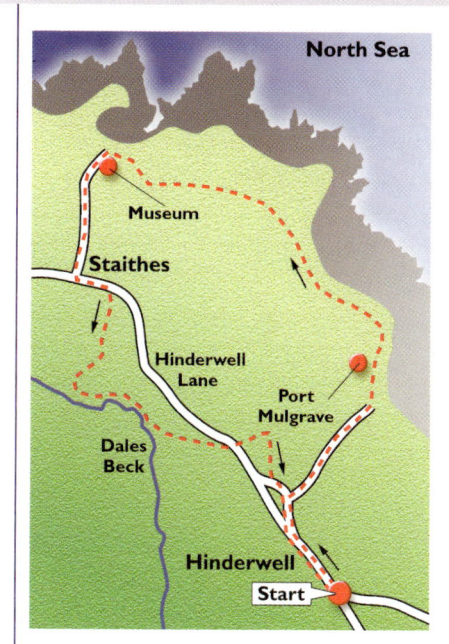

NORTH YORKSHIRE COAST

Clifftop views along the Cleveland Way

START: War memorial at south end of Hinderwell High Street.

DISTANCE: 5 miles.

GOING: Some firm pavements but also grassy stretches along clifftops and very muddy patches in woodland. Stout footwear essential.

REFRESHMENTS: Venues in Hinderwell and Staithes.

MAP: Ordnance Survey Outdoor Leisure 27 North York Moors Eastern area.

WALKS FOR ALL SEASONS **SPRING: Walk 2**

A NETWORK of footpaths links villages on the A174 with the cliff hugging Cleveland Way to give a series of magnificent views.

Starting from the war memorial at the south end of Hinderwell, we walk back along the roadway, noting the different styles of buildings and variety of materials.

When the road diverges we bear right and then right again (opposite St Hilda's Church) into Rosedale Lane. We soon pass modern properties and reach the older buildings of Port Mulgrave - with the crumbling harbour walls far below at the foot of Rosedale Cliffs.

Turning left past Nos 77 and 79 we cross a stile to follow the clifftop path towards Old Nab. Alum, jet and ironstone were quarried from the headland in earlier days and away in the distance we can make out the modern outlines of Boulby Potash Mine.

After crossing a stile, the path runs downhill beside a fence (on the right) before veering left towards Staithes. There are two more stiles as we follow the well-worn route towards farm buildings and down a stony slope that joins a stone flagged incline into Staithes.

At the bottom of the slope we pass Felicity Cottage on the left and make our way between roadside properties to reach the harbour.

The Cod And Lobster Inn is prominent as we walk through the village and up the slope past the Primitive Methodist Churches - the older church on the left dates from 1858 and the newer building of 1880 now houses a fascinating museum of local items.

Continuing up the slope above Staithes Beck, we pass the car

WALKS FOR ALL SEASONS   **SPRING: Walk 2**

Starting point: the war memorial at the south end of Hinderwell

park and Captain Cook Inn on the left hand side before reaching the junction with Whitby Road. We turn left along the A174 and, after No 42, cross a stile (on the right) into a field where we follow the fence round to the left of buildings at Seaton Hall.

After crossing stiles on either side of the farm track, we head down the field to reach a stile in the bottom right hand corner.

A short stretch of narrow pathway leads to a wide gravel area with a bridge over the beck on the left. Our route then runs away to the left up a gravel slope - with lots of long-tailed tits in nearby bushes - and, at the top of the hill, we turn left up the slope.

WALKS FOR ALL SEASONS　　　　　**SPRING: Walk 2**

Gorse bushes line the right hand side of the path and, when the path levels out, we continue along the ridge. A long series of wooden steps turns downhill through Oak Ridge Nature Reserve to reach a wooden footbridge. After crossing, we continue up a flight of wooden steps and when the path divides we follow the lower path which soon climbs to reach steps and a stile next to an old section of metalled roadway.

Turning right, we soon reach the A174 and cross with care to cross yet another stile (next to a metal field gate) before following the right-hand edge of the field to a stile.

Sailors' graves: St Hilda's churchyard at Hinderwell

There are splendid views on all sides as we make our way up the hill to a fence where a waymarker directs us away to the right. We follow the waymarked route along the top edge of the field and through a small area of woodland before heading down a short flight of steps to the public road.

We turn left for about 40 yards and then bear right up a set of steps into St Hilda's churchyard. It's worth taking a look at the striking gravestones of many local seagoing men before joining the sloping stone pavement that runs downhill to join the A174.

Then we retrace our steps through Hinderwell to our starting point.

WALKS FOR ALL SEASONS **SPRING: Walk 3**

Loftus, Hummersea and Upton

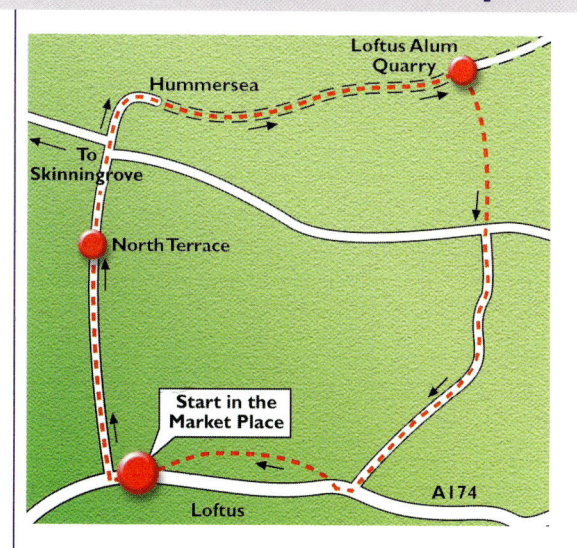

Map showing route through Loftus, North Terrace, Hummersea, Loftus Alum Quarry, with start in the Market Place, A174, and direction to Skinningrove.

<u>CLEVELAND COASTLINE</u>

In the tracks of the ironstone miners' boots

START: Loftus market place.

DISTANCE: 4 1/2 miles.

GOING: Roadways at start and finish, great care needed along cliff section.

REFRESHMENTS: Venues in Loftus.

MAP: Ordnance Survey Outdoor Leisure 27, North York Moors Eastern Area.

WALKS FOR ALL SEASONS   SPRING: Walk 3

PATHWAYS around Loftus no longer echo to the sound of ironstone miners' boots but we can still follow their routes through some spectacular coastal scenery.

Leaving the market place, we head along North Road past South View (on the left) and Cleveland Street (on the right) to follow the slope over the brow of the hill - with hedges on both sides of the roadway.

The buildings of Rose Hill Farm are away on the right as we walk towards North Terrace where we pass the buildings of Deepdale Farm (on the left) and continue directly ahead along Hummersea Lane.

From this vantage point there are spellbinding views. In the distance we can pick out the fan house on the cliff top before making our way down the slope and round the right-hand bend into Hummersea.

A wide track runs between fields and past a National Trust sign to link up with the Cleveland Way. We soon pass farm buildings on the right and after crossing a stile, the trackway threads between gorse bushes to another stile and a small wooden footbridge. From this vantage point there are spellbinding views of the coastline.

There's another stile before the pathway bears left to run uphill around the old alum quarries. At the inlet we head to the right to follow the sign to Upton and the right of way runs along the left-hand edge of the field beside the wall.

After crossing another stile (next to the metal gate) we head down the slope towards a short terrace of properties beside the public road at Upton. We turn left along the roadway but after about 15 yards our path runs away to the right beside farm buildings.

WALKS FOR ALL SEASONS   **SPRING: Walk 3**

Looking towards the alum quarry on the cliff top

There are several more stiles as we follow the right-hand field edge through a small copse and down to the roadway next to Foulsyke Farm.

At the public road (A174) we turn right to pass a stone built terrace and before the metal railings a pathway leaves the road to reach a stile. Across a short field we reach another stile and across the beck on the left there's a metal sculpture at Swalwell Wood.

A stretch of gravel pathway leads to a stile with a wooden board - 'Swalwell Wood' - and we can make out houses lining the A174 away on the left. There are two more stiles before we reach a step-over stile in the stone wall next to the red brick terraced properties on Micklow Terrace.

We walk directly ahead into East Crescent and follow the roadway round to the left where it joins Arlington Street.

Turning right, we soon pass the Arlington public house and the Primitive Methodist Chapel of 1870 before continuing up the slope to reach our starting point in the market place.

WALKS FOR ALL SEASONS **SPRING: Walk 4**

Sadberge Circular

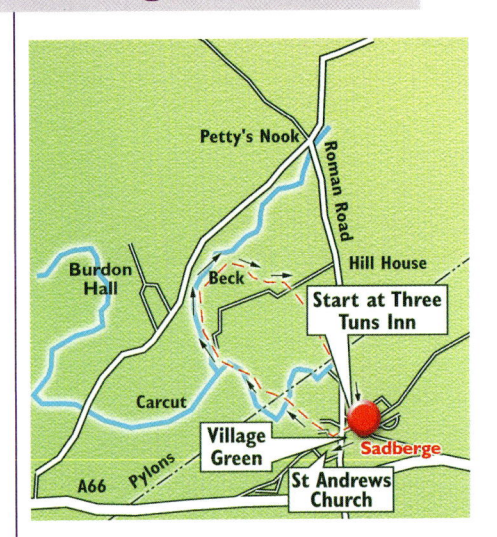

COUNTY DURHAM

Quieter times for Queen Victoria's village

START: Three Tuns Inn, Sadberge.

DISTANCE: 3¾ miles.

GOING: Mainly field paths, moderate slopes, muddy in places.

REFRESHMENTS: Three Tuns Inn or Buck Inn.

MAP: Ordnance Survey Landranger 93, Middlesbrough-Darlington.

WALKS FOR ALL SEASONS   **SPRING: Walk 4**

IN RECENT years, quieter times have returned to Sadberge but a plaque at the centre of the Green refers to Queen Victoria's title as Countess of Sadberge and gives a clue to the village's earlier importance.

Starting from the Three Tuns Inn - at one time housing the Assize Courts - we walk along Church View with St Andrew's Church on the left and Berri Cottage, Top Cottage and White House on the right.

Just before the village hall we turn right to follow the pathway that runs beside the wall and along the right hand field edge.

There are fine views away to the north-west before we reach a stile in the bottom right hand corner and the right of way

Starting point: the Three Tuns pub

then slants left across the field to a wooden footbridge. Continuing directly ahead across the next field we pass a pylon and then walk beside a hedgerow on the right to a stile.

The route is well waymarked as we make our way along the left-hand edge of the field - with a beck on the left - and after passing a small brick bridge we follow the left-hand field edge before veering right and then crossing a concrete footbridge.

Turning right, the beck is now on our right hand as we walk ahead to reach the public road. Burdon Hall is prominent on

WALKS FOR ALL SEASONS   **SPRING: Walk 4**

the hillside away to the left but we turn right along the roadway for about 40 yards before heading to the right just after a clump of trees.

The footpath turns left along the field edge - with the beck beyond the hedge on the left and a post with waymarkers soon directs us to the right up the gentle slope. Walking between fields we can see properties at Sadberge on high ground ahead.

Farm buildings at Hill House are prominent away on the left and at the top of the field we bear left and then follow a waymarker on the right of a line of posts. At the top left hand corner of the next field we cross another stile before heading left along the edge of the field.

St Andrew's Church at Sadberge

There are three more stiles as we follow the waymarker route round to the right beside a perimeter fence and then left across a field to a metal field gate.

Walking up a sloping field on the northern fringe of the village we pass through our final stile - next to another metal field gate - and continue ahead to reach the bottom end of the Green.

Our starting point at the Three Tuns is a short distance ahead on the left and if time allows, it's worth taking a closer look at some of the features that made Sadberge such an important centre in earlier days.

WALKS FOR ALL SEASONS **SPRING: Walk 5**

Stanghow and Moorsholm

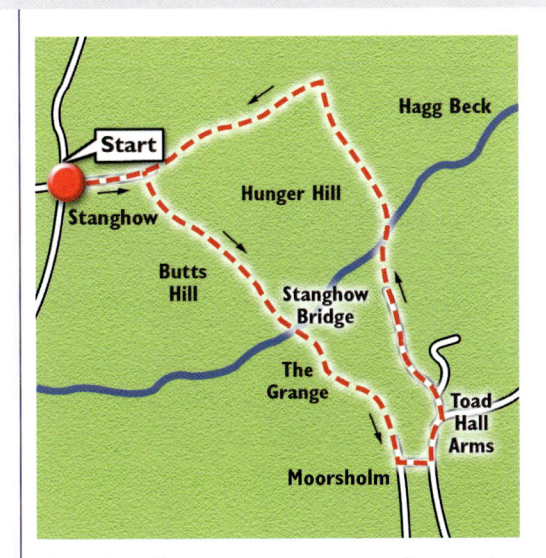

NORTH YORK MOORS

A walk on the clothery trods of old

START: Crossroads at Stanghow.

DISTANCE: 3¾ miles.

GOING: Field paths (muddy in places) with one or two moderate gradients.

REFRESHMENTS: Toad Hall Arms, Moorsholm.

MAP: Ordnance Survey Outdoor Leisure 26, North York Moors Western Area.

WALKS FOR ALL SEASONS **SPRING: Walk 5**

OVER the years a whole range of people - from churchgoers to ironstone miners - have picked their way along trods between the villages of East Cleveland.

Today these routes are little used but way-markers now guide us through countryside that offers dramatic views of coast and moorland.

Starting from the crossroads at Stanghow we head eastwards past the telephone kiosk and post box - with modern bungalows on the left. As the roadway slopes gently downhill, there are fine views of the coastline and Kilthorpe tip.

Before Low House we turn right to pass through a kissing gate and continue ahead between a stone wall on the left and wooden fence on the right.. Beyond another kissing gate we cross a section of concrete roadway to walk directly ahead - with clear views of Freeborough Hill. After a third kissing gate we continue down the sloping field to follow the right hand field edge.

Work must go on - passing a farm at Stanghow

WALKS FOR ALL SEASONS **SPRING: Walk 5**

A stile in the wire fence leads to a flight of stone steps and the path then veers to the left through woodland. More steps run down the slope to reach Stanghow Bridge and, after crossing this, the route heads out of the woodland to a wooden stile.

Continuing along the right hand field edge we soon reach another stile and walk directly ahead towards a stile in front of a barn at The Grange. We pass the farm building on the right and follow the track round to the left to join the public roadway at the centre of Moorsholm.

It's worth taking a stroll along the main road through the village before returning to the northern end. After a conversation with a couple of elderly local gents (over the garden wall, of course) I was able to locate the former police house and village school.

On to the road near Stanghow

At the northern end of Moorsholm we pass Freebrough House (with the date 1871) on the right and at the Toad Hall Arms we

Across the fields - but beware, it could be clothery

leave the road to follow a bridleway to the left. After about 90 yards we veer left on a short concrete section before joining an old stone trod that runs downhill between hedges on both sides. Another local chap had warned me that this section could be clothery ("claggy" in more local Teesside terms) and stout footwear is essential.

A cobbled stretch of track runs down to a wooden footbridge before continuing up a slope on the right and into open fields. We follow the left hand field edge directly ahead - with fine views across the coastal strip around Skinningrove away to the right.

At the end of the fields we reach a wide track that leads to Little Moorsholm Farm and at this point we turn left to make our way up the incline known as Great Charles Hill.

We soon pass an O S Triangulation Station (on the right) and follow the track past the cluster of farm buildings at Low House on the way back to our starting point at the crossroads at the centre of Stanghow.

WALKS FOR ALL SEASONS **SPRING: Walk 6**

Wensley and Bolton Hall

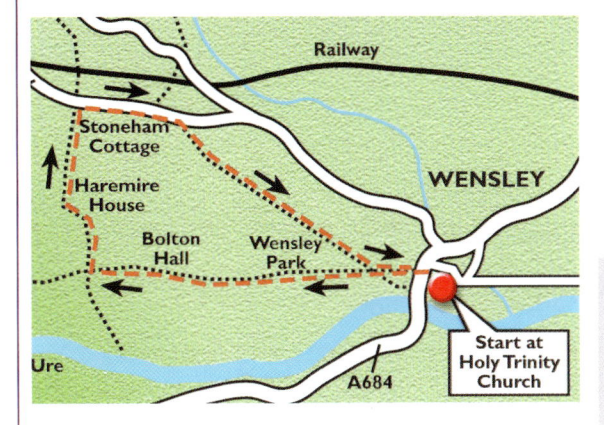

YORKSHIRE DALES

Put a walk in the Dales in your diary

START: Holy Trinity Church, Wensley.

DISTANCE: 3 1/4 miles.

GOING: One or two moderate gradients, care needed along section of road walking.

REFRESHMENTS: Venues in Leyburn.

MAP: Ordnance Survey Outdoor Leisure 30, Northern Central Areas.

WALKS FOR ALL SEASONS   **SPRING: Walk 6**

THE ATTRACTIVE village of Wensley is an ideal starting point for a stroll through nearby parkland with superb views of Wensleydale on all sides.

Holy Trinity Church has lots of interesting features including reminders of the influential Scrope family. From the churchyard we cross the village green and on the other side of the A684 we pass between impressive gate posts to make our way into Wensley Park.

The driveway runs directly ahead with parkland on both sides and fine views across West Witton away on the left. Passing Middle Lodge (on the left) we continue down a gentle slope - with lines of mature trees on both sides - and cross a small bridge with stone balustrading.

The village of Wensley

An area of pine woodland covers the sloping hillside on our right-hand side and as the drive forks we bear left down a gentle incline. The impressive frontage of Bolton Hall soon comes into view on the right. Although the interior was totally burnt out in 1902 it is possible to pick out several features of 17th century architecture.

Just past the western end of the hall we turn right along a track that runs uphill between farm buildings - with a neatly-built high stone wall on the right-hand side. When the roadway forks, we bear left and at the top of the slope there is woodland

WALKS FOR ALL SEASONS　　　　　　**SPRING: Walk 6**

The church at Wensley has lots of interesting features, including reminders of the Scrope family

close at hand on the left and a high hedge on the right. Following the track round to the right there are hedges on both sides and, as the slope runs uphill, we can see Haremire House across the field on the left. At the top of the slope the trackway passes between woodland and runs through to join the public roadway opposite Stoneham Cottage.

We turn right along the road which runs gently downhill - with the buildings of Tullis Cote coming into view on the left. Reaching an area of woodland on the right, we turn right and after about 50 yards the track forks. At this point we bear left and cross a cattle grid as we leave the woodland before following the trackway around the perimeter of the wooded area.

Before the next cattle grid (just before the house) we bear left and then follow the wall round to the right to pass through a field gate. Continuing between fences, we head diagonally left down the sloping field towards a mature tree in the middle of the parkland.

Our route runs down the field towards a metal field gate that leads to the driveway through Wensley Park. After passing through, we turn left to retrace our steps back into Wensley village.

The impressive gateposts which lead the way into Wensley Park

Enjoying summer's glories

THE longer daylight hours of summer offer the chance to explore routes that are a little further from the beaten path - whether they are on the moor tops or in the deeply-wooded valleys of East Cleveland or Eskdale.

The early months of summer bring the glorious boughs of apple blossom, flowering cherry and hawthorn flowers and during mid-summer one of the great joys of the countryside are the spreading fields of poppies.

Even during the summer months it is important to set out with the proper clothing and footwear to avoid being caught out by rapid changes in the summer-time weather. Wear a hat to protect from the sun's harmful rays and remember to take sun-block or lotion with you.

Walks in this section are a little more demanding in terms of distance and difficulty of terrain - in particular the slopes and woodland between Easington and Roxby, where steep gradients and slippery surfaces can cause problems.

A variety of landscapes on these walks includes the contrasting natural beauty of moorland and this section includes one of my all-time favourite routes between those lovely North Yorkshire villages of Lastingham and Hutton le Hole.

WALKS FOR ALL SEASONS — **SUMMER: Walk 1**

Clay Bank and Greenhow

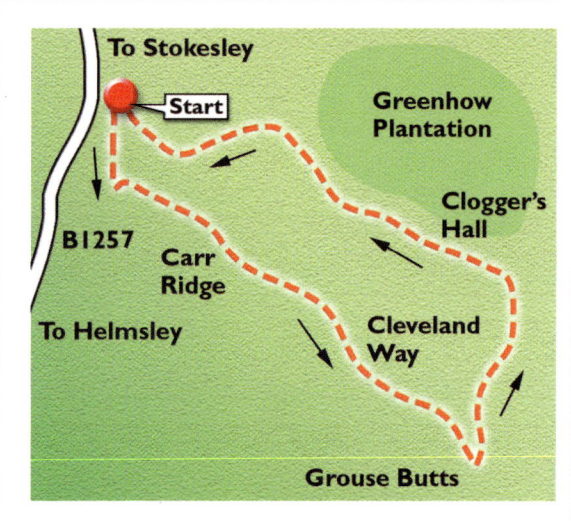

(Map showing route from Start at car park on B1257 near To Stokesley, passing Carr Ridge, Greenhow Plantation, Clogger's Hall, Cleveland Way, Grouse Butts, with To Helmsley to the southwest.)

Walk Facts

NORTH YORK MOORS

Corner of contrasts on the Way

START: Car park on Clay Bank (B1257 south of Great Broughton).

DISTANCE: 3 1/2 miles.

GOING: Steep gradients and rough track in places.

REFRESHMENTS: Nearest venues in Great Broughton or Ingleby Greenhow.

MAP: Ordnance Survey Outdoor Leisure 26, North York Moors Western Area.

WALKS FOR ALL SEASONS **SUMMER: Walk 1**

THE north-eastern corner of the North York Moors has some superb contrasts - from high moorland to man-made plantations and lowland views - and the car park on Clay Bank is an ideal starting point for this scenic circuit.

From the car park we walk southwards along the B1257 towards Bilsdale and, after the name plate on the left hand side, the well worn route of the Cleveland Way starts beyond the gate.

Cleveland Way

Heading up the steps, we soon reach a grassy stretch - with a plantation close at hand on the left.

There are some fine views from Bilsdale away to the right and, after passing through another gate, we continue up the slope and leave the plantation behind. Beyond yet another gate, we continue directly ahead at the signpost along a level gravel pathway (with narrow drainage channels running diagonally across the route at regular intervals).

The track then rises gently before levelling out and at the next signpost we bear left away from the Cleveland Way. Away to the right we can make out the cliff faces close to Botton Head but, as we head northwards, Roseberry Topping and the tall chimneys of industrial Teesside stand out on the skyline.

Continuing down the slope we cross a gulley (running left to right) and at the sign our route runs directly ahead. Care is needed down Jackson's Bank where the path runs through a rocky gulley between boulders on both sides to end at a field gate.

WALKS FOR ALL SEASONS **SUMMER: Walk 1**

The view from the top of Clay Bank

Beyond this gate we walk directly ahead to a junction of paths where we bear right for about 30 yards and then left down a grassy slope.

At the next junction of paths we head left up the slope and, when a path joins from the left, we continue directly ahead through the Greenhow Plantation.

This wide, level path is muddy in places and as it bends and rises gently there are silver birches on the left hand side.

We soon reach two view points on the right hand side - the second one with seats - and it's worth pausing to take in the lovely landscape views between Ingleby Greenhow and Great Broughton. The path then veers away to the right to join a stony section that leads to a roadside gate.

After crossing the stile we bear right along the B1257 and make our way down the slope to the car park where it's worth taking in some superb views across lower ground towards Teesside and spending some time thinking about the Bronze Age cemetery and crematorium that was uncovered by accident in 1969.

WALKS FOR ALL SEASONS — **SUMMER: Walk 2**

Cringle Moor Circular

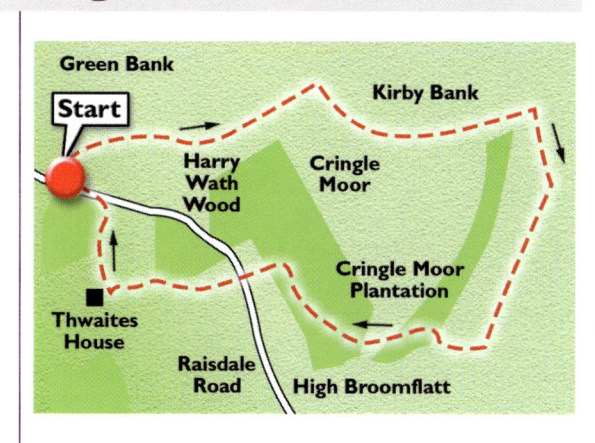

Map showing the circular route with labels: Green Bank, Start, Kirby Bank, Harry Wath Wood, Cringle Moor, Cringle Moor Plantation, Thwaites House, Raisdale Road, High Broomflatt.

Walk Facts

<u>NORTH YORKSHIRE</u>

A view across the Yorkshire landscape

START: Lord Stones Cafe, top of Carlton Bank.

DISTANCE: 3 3/4 miles.

GOING: Fairly rough in places with moderate inclines.

REFRESHMENTS: Lord Stones Cafe.

MAP: Ordnance Survey Outdoor Leisure 26, North York Moors Western Area.

WALKS FOR ALL SEASONS **SUMMER: Walk 2**

THE LORD Stones Cafe at the top of Carlton Bank is an ideal starting point for exploring the varied countryside south of the Cleveland Way.

Walking through the car park (away from the road) we pass a clump of trees dedicated to Alec and Annie Falconer and then bear right to follow the main track beside a wire fence.

The pathway slopes gently downhill before rising between a stone wall and wire fence to reach a wooden gate that leads to a flagged section of the route.

Heather moorland spreads away to the right as we make the steep climb along the next stretch and it's worth pausing to take in some fine views looking back.

The trees dedicated to Alec and Annie Falconer

At the top of the climb we reach a view point where the track veers to the right along the ridge and there are superb views of the North Yorkshire landscape from this section.

The next section is quite demanding as we make our way down a steep slope with uneven, stony areas underfoot. At the foot of the hill we turn to the right (away from the Cleveland Way) along a pathway between spoil heaps.

After passing through a gate we walk beside a stone wall before bearing to the right to join a narrow pathway that threads its

WALKS FOR ALL SEASONS   **SUMMER: Walk 2**

Walkers approach the Lord Stones cafe on Carlton Bank

way along the slope - with spoil heaps lining the hillside on our right. Farm buildings at Beak Hills are prominent away on the left as we head towards a field gate, but a waymarker (before the gate) directs us away to the right alongside a wire fence.

The pathway winds up the hillside to reach the eastern edge of Cringle Moor Plantation and, after crossing the stile into the woodland, we follow a dark tunnel between tall evergreen trees. The next stile leads to an open area and, after crossing, we reach a wooden field gate that opens into a wide trackway running through the forest. Bearing to the right along the track, we soon reach a straight stretch - with a post and waymarker directing us away to the left.

The track soon runs down the slope to the edge of the wood where we turn left and continue along the field edge as it runs down to the roadway. After crossing, we head through the gate and down the field to reach a plank bridge where we turn left to cross a stile. Turning left we continue down the slope and, after crossing the beck, there are two stiles as we approach Thwaites House.

A welcome cuppa at the cafe

Walking directly ahead - with the buildings of Thwaites House on the left - we pass through a gate that leads to a track where we turn right. After crossing a stile next to the wooden field gate and making our way through a metal field gate we reach the public roadway at Raisdale Road.

We turn left to walk the short distance back along the metalled road to our starting point at the Lord Stones Cafe where parking is free if any purchase is made.

WALKS FOR ALL SEASONS **SUMMER: Walk 3**

Easington and Roxby

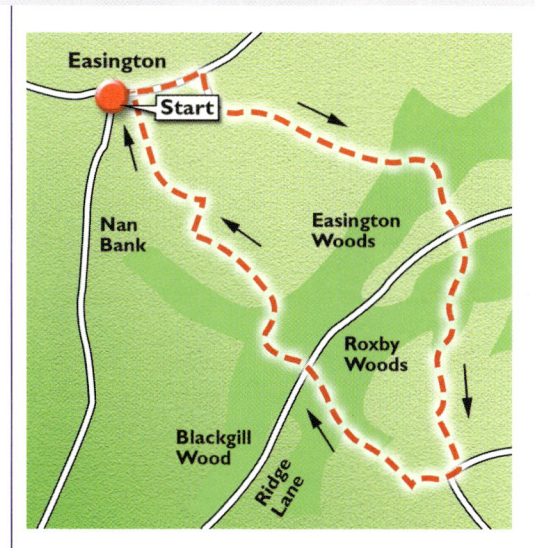

EAST CLEVELAND

The manor houses and the potash mine

START: At All Saints' Church on Whitby Road (A174), Easington.

DISTANCE: 5$\frac{1}{2}$ miles.

GOING: Mixture of field paths, firm tracks and very muddy, steep slopes in woodland areas. Stout footwear essential.

REFRESHMENTS: Venues in Easington.

MAP: Ordnance Survey Outdoor Leisure 27 North York Moors Eastern Area.

WALKS FOR ALL SEASONS **SUMMER: Walk 3**

ROLLING countryside between Loftus and Staithes has lots of industrial settings and the site of important medieval manor houses at Easington and Roxby - but the route between the two villages crosses two wooded valleys and stout footwear is essential.

Starting from Easington's Church of All Saints, we head eastwards along the A174 and soon pass White House and Arglam Farm on the right (across the road behind Easington Hall Farm is the site of the Conyers family's manor house).

We follow the grass verge as far as the track on the right that runs towards Twizziegill Farm and, just before the farm buildings, we turn left to follow the waymarkers over two stiles and around the buildings

The view from Roxby

before heading to the left along the field edge.

There are dramatic views of the Boulby Potash Mine from this high point before we cross a stile (on the right) to follow the field edge down the slope and over the railway line.

Walking directly ahead into Mines Wood, we follow the main

WALKS FOR ALL SEASONS   **SUMMER: Walk 3**

The view of Boulby Potash Mine from Roxby

pathway down a very slippery slope and into an open area where we turn left down the gentle incline before heading away to the right towards a way-marked post.

We make our way up the slope through the woodland and, after crossing a stile, our route runs across the field to another stile and out on to the public road.

Turning right along the roadway, we pass farm buildings (on the left) and then cross a stile on the left (immediately after the farm) to head down the field into Roxby Woods.

A wooden footbridge crosses Roxby Beck and we then head over a stile into a large field. Keeping to the right hand side of the field, our route runs through a metal field gate and along a gravel track that swings to the left and up the slope to reach the public roadway close to Roxby Church.

Passing the church (and site of the Boynton family's manor house) on our right, we leave the road on the bend to follow the stony track towards Little Wood. Waymarkers direct us through a metal field gate and, as the track turns to the right, we head left over a stile into the woodland.

More waymarkers guide us first to the right and then left at a large tree before the path wends its way through the woods to reach a wide trackway.

After crossing this track, we make our way over the footbridge that spans Roxby Beck and continue up the slope to reach Ridge Lane. We head left for about ten yards and then leave the roadway by following the pathway on the right into woodland.

The path soon runs down a steep slope before a waymarker directs us away to the left - with pheasants, squirrels and a deer for company on my recent visit.

Crossing a wide track, we follow a grassy track to a stile where the right of way crosses the railway line to reach a flight of steps a few yards to the right. Continuing up the slope to cross a stile, we follow the right-hand field edge for three field lengths (passing a track on the right to Twizziegill Farm) before turning right along the field edge.

Halfway along the field we cross two stiles and then turn left along the field edge to cross another stile. At this point we bear diagonally to the right to cross yet another stile in the wire fence before turning right down the grassy slope.

The route runs directly ahead through an extremely muddy area as we approach the buildings at Arglam Farm and through the farmyard to join the A174 at the eastern end of Easington.

Turning left along the roadway, we make our way back past the White House to our starting point at All Saints' Church.

WALKS FOR ALL SEASONS **SUMMER: Walk 4**

Lastingham and Hutton le Hole

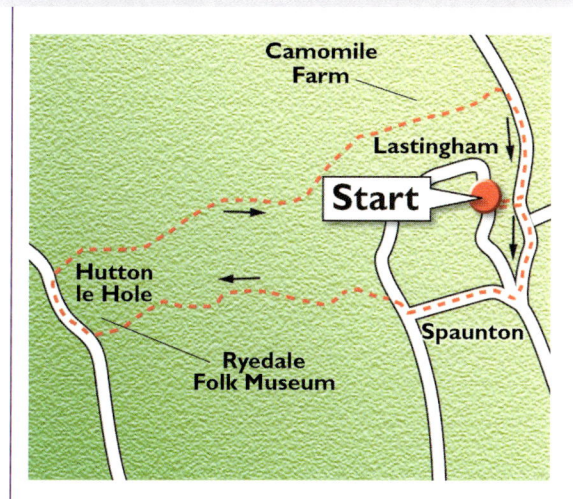

Map showing route between Lastingham, Camomile Farm, Hutton le Hole, Ryedale Folk Museum and Spaunton, with Start at Lastingham.

<u>NORTH YORK MOORS</u>

Paradise found in North Yorkshire

START: Blacksmith's Arms, Lastingham.

DISTANCE: 4¾ miles.

GOING: Several moderate gradients.

REFRESHMENTS: Blacksmith's Arms, Lastingham and venues in Hutton le Hole.

MAP: Ordnance Survey Outdoor Leisure 26, North York Moors Western Area.

WALKS FOR ALL SEASONS — SUMMER: Walk 4

A gentle stroll through glorious scenery between two of Yorkshire's prettiest villages- that's my idea of paradise and it's only about 25 miles from central Teesside!

Starting from the Blacksmith's Arms at Lastingham we bear left past Fern Cottage and The Green before crossing the bridge close to St Cedd's Well (on the left). Bearing to the right through the village, the Wesleyan Chapel is on the left and as the main road bends to the left we turn right to cross Jackson Bridge.

Walking beside the beck, there are stone built cottages on the right and, after the garages, we walk up the grassy slope into the woodland. The path runs directly ahead before veering to the left with a gulley close at hand on the right.

We pass through a gate at the top of the slope and follow a level stretch through to the public road where we turn right and almost immediately left towards Spaunton. Walking through the scattered hamlet of Spaunton, we turn right at the junction and then bear left away from the public roadway (beside a cattle grid) on the approach to Grange Farm. A concrete track veers to the right and we then turn right after the barn along a stony track between fences. Continuing up the slope towards farm buildings, the track bears left and then right (with a broken down wall on the right) before running left down another slope to pass through a gap in the wall.

The next section of the route runs through woodland - with glimpses of Hutton le Hole through the trees - and then continues diagonally to the left to pass through a metal field gate which leads into another belt of woodland. There's another stile (and gate) as we walk beside the beck and through to the public roadway. We turn right along the road and soon pass Burnley House (on the left) with St Chad's Church set back from the roadway on the right.

It's easy to see why Hutton le Hole is often described as one of Yorkshire's prettiest villages and, after savouring the atmosphere or paying a visit to the splendid Ryedale Folk Museum, we leave the village by following a footpath that runs on the south side of the museum area.

The path skirts around wooden sheds and, after crossing a stile, it runs alongside the museum field. After veering left, there are three more stiles before we cross a footbridge. Continuing ahead through woodland, we pass through a field gate to walk beside the roadway which soons dips past High Cross House (on the right). Just before the bridge, we bear left on a track that runs beside allotments and over a narrow beck before veering to the right across the moor.

Hutton le Hole

As we approach Camomile Farm the right of way swings left to run close to the trees and we then follow the wall downhill to cross Hole Beck. Walking up the hillside we pass through two kissing gates and at the signposts we turn right to make our way down the slope past Lastingham Grange Hotel into the village.

At the junction we bear right to re-cross the road bridge and our starting point at the Blacksmith's Arms is round the corner on the right.

WALKS FOR ALL SEASONS **SUMMER: Walk 5**

Littlebeck and Falling Foss

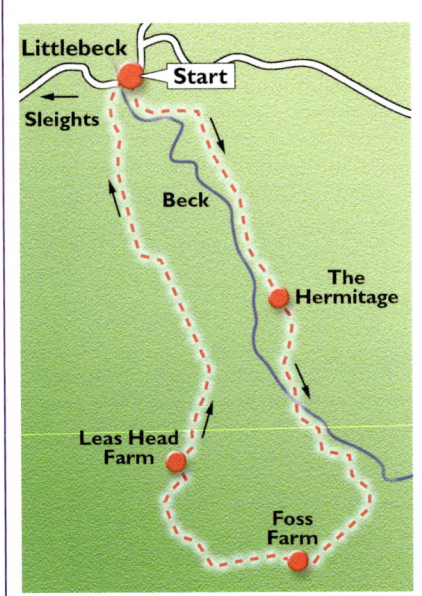

Map shows route from Start at Littlebeck, past Beck, The Hermitage, Foss Farm, and Leas Head Farm. Sleights lies to the west.

NORTH YORK MOORS

Walking to the waterfalls of Foss

Walk Facts

START: Littlebeck village hall (two miles south-east of Sleights - off A169).

DISTANCE: 4 miles.

GOING: Some moderate slopes and uneven surfaces in woodland stretches leading to Falling Foss (severe slope on roadway at start/finish).

REFRESHMENTS: Several venues in Sleights.

MAP: OS Outdoor Leisure 27. North York Moors Eastern Area.

WALKS FOR ALL SEASONS   SUMMER: Walk 5

TUCKED away in delightful locations on the North York Moors are a number of dramatic waterfalls - usually linked to nearby villages by leafy routes through swathes of woodland.

Starting from the village hall at Littlebeck (near Sleights) we walk down the tarmac roadway and, at the left-hand bend before the bottom of the hill, we turn left through a wooden kissing gate.

As we follow the path between trees, the beck is on our right and along a cobbled section the land drops away steeply (on the right) before climbing gently through the woodland.

The route soon swings to the right to run along a stretch with wooden rails. After bearing to the left, the track runs to the right up a flight of steps - with shale tips on the right.

Veering gently to the right, a flight of steps runs down the incline and the track is uneven in places as it rises and falls over networks of tree roots.

A long flight of stone steps runs uphill and at the top of the slope is the Hermitage - with the detail "GC 1790" above the doorway to the cave.

Keeping to the higher path, a waymarked post then directs us on the C to C route away to the right and along a railed section high above the valley.

We soon make our way down a flight of steps to view Falling Foss and the adjacent stone building before following the main pathway over a wooden footbridge.

Keeping to the right of the single-arched stone bridge we follow the track up the slope to a wide lane where we turn right on the bridleway that passes woodland on the left and fields on the right.

WALKS FOR ALL SEASONS **SUMMER: Walk 5**

The waterfall at Falling Foss

WALKS FOR ALL SEASONS   **SUMMER: Walk 5**

The old Hermitage near Falling Foss

Continuing directly ahead past farm buildings on the right, the wide track veers round to the right - with a hedge on the left and wire fence on the right.

At the gates there are three signposts and we turn right to make our way down the field alongside a hedge on our left hand side. We reach a gate with a notice "Leashead" and, after crossing a concrete bridge, we head up a stony path before turning left before the buildings.

Beyond the stile we reach a track that runs to the left up to a metal gate where we turn immediately right along the track with a fence on our right.

Passing through another metal gate, we continue directly ahead with a wire fence on the left and our way-marked route then passes through three wooden gates to reach the Little Beck Nature Reserve where oak trees grow among areas of scrub and grassland.

The path runs through woodland and down a slope - with steps at the lower level - before crossing a beck just before the public roadway. The Methodist Chapel is on the left, but we turn right along the roadway. After crossing the ford, we continue up the hill and round the bend to return to our starting point.

WALKS FOR ALL SEASONS **SUMMER: Walk 6**

Old Byland and Tylas Farm

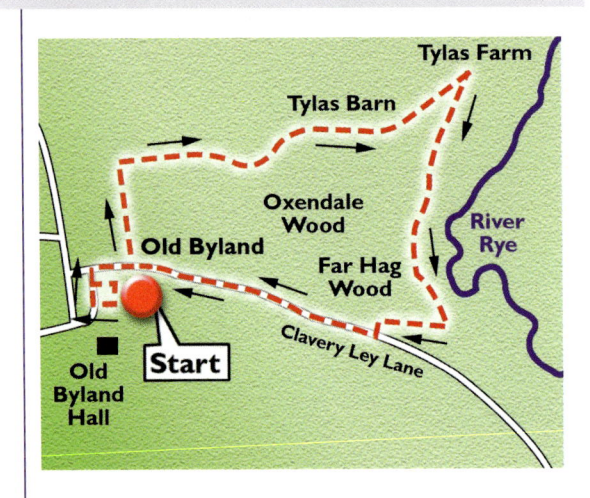

NORTH YORK MOORS

The old religious houses of Ryedale

START: Old Byland Church.

DISTANCE: 3 1/2 miles.

GOING: One or two moderate slopes, otherwise fairly level.

REFRESHMENTS: Nearest venues in Helmsley or Sutton Bank, NY Moors Centre.

MAP: Ordnance Survey Outdoor Leisure 26, North York Moors Western Area.

WALKS FOR ALL SEASONS **SUMMER: Walk 6**

THE tiny village of Old Byland (two miles west of Rievaulx) has a fine little church and links with the two nearby abbeys of Rievaulx and Byland.

A Saxon sundial on the eastern side of the porch reminds us of the early church building and among the interesting interior features are carved human heads (with rams' horns) on the Norman chancel arch.

Monks moved local folk into the village from a nearby site (now Tylas Farm) as part of a short-lived plan to build an abbey. They were soon moved on by clergy who were already based at Rievaulx Abbey and finally settled at Byland Abbey.

From the church we return to The Green and walk northwards up the slope before turning right at the junction.

There are farm buildings on both sides of the roadway, but we soon head left over a ladder stile into the field and continue directly ahead through a gap in the hedge.

A sign at the end of the next field directs us away to the right and we cross three stiles before joining a stony track that runs directly ahead with a deep gulley (caused by quarry workings) close at hand on the right.

We can pick out Rievaulx Abbey in a lovely setting among trees away to the right and, after passing Tylas Barn (on the left), we pass through a field gate to follow the stony slope downhill.

The buildings of Tylas Farm are all that is left of the earlier village and, just before the farmstead, we bear right on a tarmac roadway that bends down the slope with the River Rye close at hand on the left.

There are lovely views of Ryedale's wooded slopes as the roadway rises and falls towards Rievaulx. A footpath runs away to the left but we keep to the metalled road as we head towards

WALKS FOR ALL SEASONS   **SUMMER: Walk 6**

Lambert Hag Wood (on the right).

Just before the cattle grid (and woodland), we leave the road and bear right up the sloping hillside.

Passing through a collection of silver birch trees, we keep to the left hand side of the slope and, when we reach the ridge, a signpost is clearly visible in the hedgerow away on the left.

A stile leads to the roadway where we turn right to follow Clavery Ley Lane directly ahead between fields on both sides.

We can make out the wooded slopes above Low Gill on the left and it's a level route ... but then there's always the unexpected! On my recent visit, a large herd of dairy cattle (accompanied by prize bull) emerged from a field on the right and slowed my pace!

Buildings on the eastern edge of Old Byland soon come into view and, at the road junction, we turn left to retrace our route back to the Church of All Saints.

Tylas Farm, between Old Byland and Revaulx

Mists and mellow fruitfulness

IN the words of John Keats, autumn is the "season of mists and mellow fruitfulness" and, for me, one of the most abiding memories of the year is the contrasting browns, yellows and golds of woodlands and valleys.

Beeches, oaks and chestnuts provide food for squirrels and other creatures. Hawthorn berries are popular with birds while we humans can gather the berries from bramble bushes as filling for delicious home-made pies.

With the onset of shorter daylight hours and colder winds, it becomes even more important to carry extra layers of warm or waterproof clothing and hot drinks and to allow ample time to complete the walk during day time.

This is probably a good time of year to explore the landscape at a slightly lower level and, in addition to well-known areas of the North York Moors, I have included routes through interesting and attractive countryside to the south of Durham City at Sunderland Bridge and Hett Village. A place with such a curious name deserves further investigation and a closer look at this area of South Durham soon shows the dramatic changes that have taken place since the coal-mining era.

WALKS FOR ALL SEASONS **AUTUMN: Walk 1**

Castleton Circular

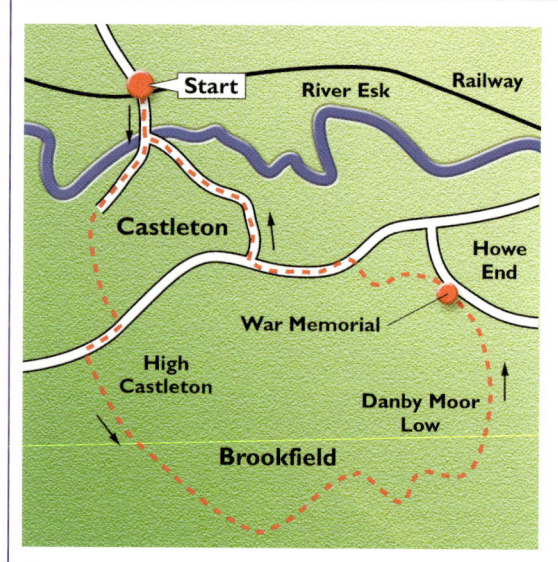

Eskdale

Letting the train take the strain

START: Castleton Station.

DISTANCE: 3½ miles.

GOING: Some firm pavements around Castleton as well as field paths. One or two moderate gradients.

REFRESHMENTS: Several venues in Castleton.

MAP: Ordnance Survey Outdoor Leisure 26, North York Moors Western Area.

WALKS FOR ALL SEASONS **AUTUMN: Walk 1**

THE Middlesbrough-Whitby rail link offers the chance to leave the car at home and explore superb areas of countryside close to stations on the route through Eskdale.

Starting from Castleton railway station, we turn right along the public road to pass under the bridge and close to the Eskdale Inn (on the right). Just beyond the road bridge over the River Esk, we turn right along the metalled roadway towards Westerdale and soon pass Esk Mill on the right.

At the end of the stone wall on the left-hand side of the road, we turn left to follow the track that runs up the hillside and, as we reach the top half of the slope, the pathway bends to the left before joining the roadway opposite the Moorlands Hotel.

Turning right up the hill, we soon leave the roadway to follow the lane that runs downhill towards Didderhowe Farm. The track continues between stone walls and over a cattle grid before passing to the left of the farm buildings.

The bridge on the Esk

After crossing a stile, we make our way directly ahead across the field to reach another stile on the left of a metal field gate. Continuing along the left hand edge of the field, we cross another stile on the right of the field gate then, just beyond the beck, we turn left (away from the Esk Valley Walkway).

Passing through a field gate, we walk directly ahead before bearing left down the grassy slope to reach another field gate.

After crossing the beck, we bear right (with a wooden fence on the left) and soon reach a small gate. Waymarkers guide us to the left (through another gate) and up a slope to the roadway.

We turn right along the metalled road and, at the wooden field gate, our route turns left (away from the road) towards Danby Low Moor. When the path splits, we turn right to follow the well-marked track that runs around the moor top before joining the metalled roadway close to Howe Cottage.

Walking to the left along the road, we soon reach the junction (with the Ainthorpe Road) and almost immediately turn left again along the lower pathway that runs below the war memorial. The track continues down the grassy slope to a set of wooden railings and, after crossing a stone bridge, we continue between stone walls to join the public road opposite the Church of St George and St Michael.

We turn left up the roadway and soon pass Castle Close and Apple Tree House (on the right) before joining the High Street in the centre of Castleton.

In the heart of Castleton

At the Downe Arms we cross the road and turn right next to No2 Wayside to follow the path away from the stone-built cottages and down the slope - with Castle Hill across the road on the right. Passing the play area at the bottom of the hill, we turn right to make our way over the road bridge and back past the Eskdale Hotel to our starting point.

WALKS FOR ALL SEASONS **AUTUMN: Walk 2**

Great Ayton & Holme's Bridge

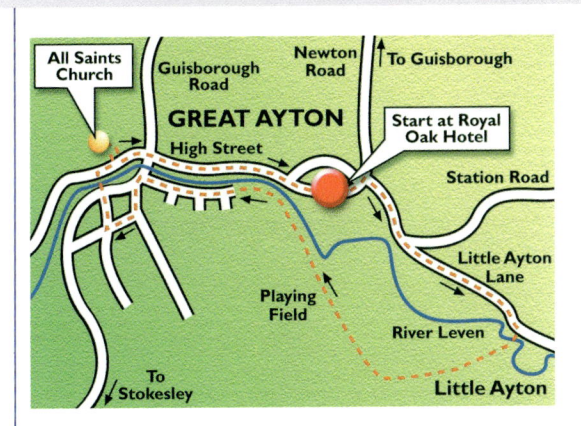

<u>NORTH YORK MOORS</u>

The friendly village with a Quaker past

START: Royal Oak Hotel, Great Ayton.

DISTANCE: 2 1/2 miles.

GOING: Mainly level field sections, may be muddy.

REFRESHMENTS: Several venues in Great Ayton.

MAP: Ordnance Survey Outdoor Leisure 26 North York Moors Western Area or Middlesbrough A-Z, page 120.

WALKS FOR ALL SEASONS   AUTUMN: Walk 2

THERE is so much happening in Great Ayton that I have to make regular visits to keep up with all the changes - which make the village even more attractive.

Starting from the Royal Oak Hotel on the High Green we cross the road with care to pass the car park and tourist information office on the right hand side and then turn right into Little Ayton Lane.

New housing covers ground on the former Friends School site and, as the road divides, we bear right to cross Leven Court.

We continue up the gentle slope between hedges on both sides of the roadway and soon pass houses on the right hand side.

Just past a seat (on the right) we turn right along a footpath that leads to Holme's Bridge.

It's worth pausing on the footbridge to take a look at the natural beauty along the River Leven before bearing to the right across the large field.

We pass through a gap next to a large holly bush and continue to the left to reach a step-through stile. A clearly marked track leads to another gap in the hedge and the right of way then runs along the right-hand edge of the field.

Walking directly ahead, we pass the football field and then the cricket field (on the left) and the pathway then turns close to the River Leven on the approach to a weir.

Just before the kissing gate near the river, we turn left to make our way along the bottom edge of the field and another kissing gate leads into Hollygarth - with the river close at hand on the right.

We walk along the front of the buildings and at the entrance to Hollygarth Close a track leads directly ahead - with a fence on the left and holly hedge on the right.

WALKS FOR ALL SEASONS **AUTUMN: Walk 2**

Ducks enjoy a cooling paddle in the River Leven at Great Ayton

We soon reach the roadway at Bridge Street - with the obelisk marking the site of James Cook's home close at hand - and cross with care into Mill Terrace.

Following the roadway round to the right into West Terrace, we pass the Buck Inn and after crossing Levenside we make our way over the wooden footbridge that spans the Leven and then turn right along Low Green.

It's worth making the short detour to take a closer look at All Saints' Church and, after returning to Low Green, we follow the roadway towards the road bridge .

Marwood School is prominent beside the road and after crossing with care we follow the High Street directly ahead - with the

WALKS FOR ALL SEASONS   **AUTUMN: Walk 2**

Congregational Church building (1879) on the right. We soon cross Beech Close (on the left) and, after passing the modern Methodist Church, there is quite a contrast in the form of the red-brick village hall.

On the corner of Park Rise, the Captain Cook Schoolroom Museum is worth a closer look and a little further along the sloping High Street, the former village school now houses the village's library.

Following the High Street round to the left, we reach the High Green - with the statue of young James Cook - and our starting point at the Royal Oak is close at hand on the left.

The former village school - now the public library

WALKS FOR ALL SEASONS **AUTUMN: Walk 3**

Hett Circular

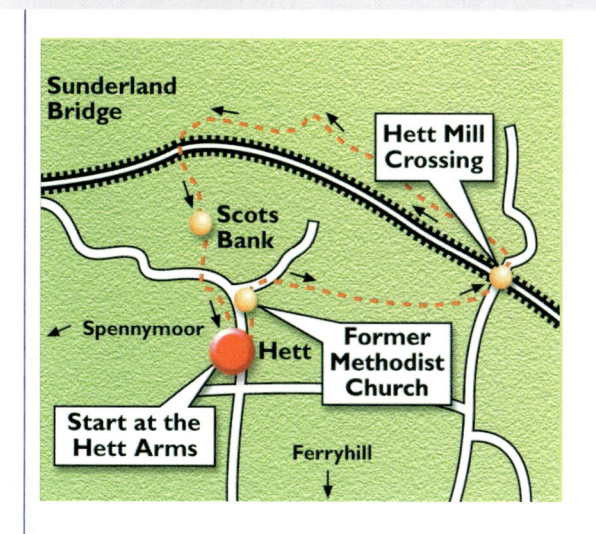

COUNTY DURHAM

An oasis between road and railway

START: Hett Arms, Hett (west of A167, four miles south of Durham City).

DISTANCE: 3¾ miles.

GOING: Incline at Scots Bank, woodland paths may be muddy.

REFRESHMENTS: Hett Arms.

MAP: Ordnance Survey Landranger 93, Middlesbrough and Darlington area.

WALKS FOR ALL SEASONS   AUTUMN: Walk 3

SET in the east Durham landscape between Croxdale and Coxhoe, the tiny village of Hett is an ideal starting point for exploring the rolling countryside that lies close to the River Wear.

Starting from the Hett Arms at the centre of the village, we walk northwards past a row of modern properties on the left and a football pitch on the right.

We soon reach High Grange Farm on the left and bear right to cross the road towards the north-east corner of the village. Following a footpath next to the former chapel, we walk between hedges - catching sight of the tower of Durham Cathedral and Penshaw Monument away on the left hand distance. The township of Coxhoe is directly ahead as we reach a stile and after crossing we walk diagonally to the right through the field towards the hedgerow.

We turn left along the field edge as far as another stile (opposite the line of the hedge on the left) and bear left around the next field before crossing two more stiles as the well-marked route runs downhill through the fields.

We can clearly see traffic on the A1(M) in the distance and the main east coast railway line curves through countryside closer at hand. The pathway reaches the public roadway close to the level crossing at Hett Mill and after making our way over the track we pass a large roadside property.

Continuing over the bridge, we immediately turn left on the path beside the beck as it rises gently between hawthorn and elderberry bushes.

There are gorse bushes on the right hand side as the path rises and falls beside the beck - with the railway embankment high above the beck on the left.

A woodland trail between Hett and Croxdale

The pathway runs through delightful woodland but it is very muddy in places and stout footwear is essential.

After crossing a wooden footbridge, we walk up the slope which has a wooden seat on the right. A flight of wooden steps leads up the bankside between silver birches and out of the woodland to turn left along the field edge for about 50 yards

WALKS FOR ALL SEASONS **AUTUMN: Walk 3**

before heading back into the woodland down a flight of wooden steps and over a footbridge.

We turn left to follow the field edge - with pine trees on the left hand side - and we can pick out housing at Brandon directly ahead. As the path veers to the right around the field edge, we cross a stile in the fence on the left and turn left along a wide pathway with wire fences on both sides.

At the bottom of the slope we cross a water-course and, after crossing the stile, we walk up the left hand field edge to a ladder stile. The pathway then runs to the left (with a wire fence on the right) to reach a concrete footbridge with metal rails.

Hett Mill railway crossing

After crossing the stile we continue straight up the field known as Scots Bank (the name is said to be linked with the massacre of Scottish forces after the battle of Neville's Cross in 1346). There are gorse bushes on the left as we continue uphill towards farm buildings and through to the public road.

Turning left along the roadway, we walk back into Hett and our starting point at the Hett Arms is on the right at the centre of the village.

WALKS FOR ALL SEASONS   **AUTUMN: Walk 4**

Lealholm South

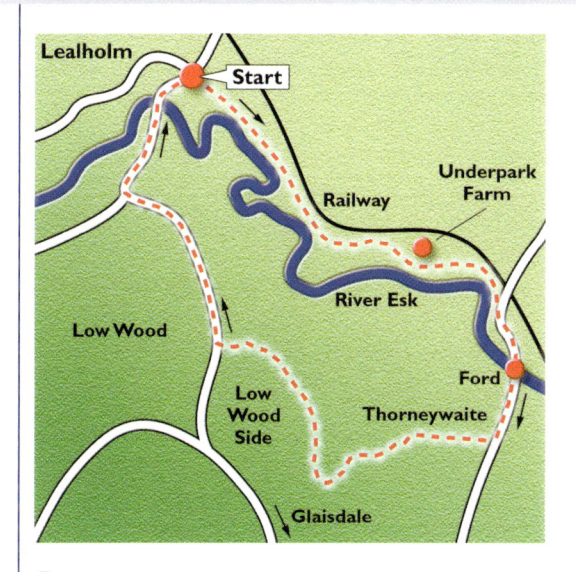

Eskdale

Lealholm is where the heart is

START: Car park next to Lealholm School.

DISTANCE: 3¼ miles

GOING: Some moderate gradients, muddy and slippery areas need care.

REFRESHMENTS: Venues in Lealholm.

MAP: Ordance Survey Outdoor Leisure 27, North York Moors Eastern Area.

WALKS FOR ALL SEASONS   **AUTUMN: Walk 4**

MOST public roads through Eskdale keep to higher ground and the best way to explore this glorious river-side scenery is by rail or on foot.

Starting from the car park next to the village school, we turn left along the Esk Valley Walk and pass stone cottages on our right-hand side. The railway line runs along the ridge on the left and we soon pass Esk Close on the right.

The wide trackway dips downhill to run beside the River Esk before rising again - with some fine views away to the right. After a left hand bend we can see the buildings of Underpark Farm directly ahead and the route then swings to the right.

Soon after crossing a very muddy stretch we reach a stile next to a metal gate at the end of farm buildings and the right of way then follows the right hand field edge alongside the Esk.

There is some scenery to savour on this stretch of riverbank and, after crossing an outfall, we make our way up a short slope to cross a stile in the wooden fence. From this point a wooden footbridge runs along a stone-built embankment next to the railway line on the left hand side.

The railway bridge is close at hand on the left as our route veers to the right to join a wide trackway. Continuing down the slope, you may just spot the heron that was on the riverbank on my recent visit. After the next left hand bend, we turn right over a wooden footbridge (before the ford and railway bridge).

We make our way up the stone bank and soon pass a stone-built property, Rake Cottage, on the left to reach a section of tarmac roadway. There are superb views away to the left past Thorneywaite and we soon turn right (opposite the last road-side building) to follow the driveway that leads to High Brock Rigg.

Just before the stone buildings we turn left down a stone trod

WALKS FOR ALL SEASONS   **AUTUMN: Walk 4**

(but beware of the slippery surface!) and, at the bottom of the slope, we reach a wooden field gate - with a pond on the right.

After passing a gate and stile on the left, we continue directly ahead with the beck close at hand on the right.

We continue along the main pathway between hedges to reach a wooden field gate and, when the paths divide, we keep left to cross a stony track.

Passing a bungalow on the right, we soon reach Laneside and Beckside Cottage on the right and at the public road we turn right past Hall Garth and Byre Cottage.

Lealholm village, looking towards the River Esk

The roadway runs round to the right downhill and over a stone bridge before climbing uphill past Meadowfield and a terrace of stone-built cottages before the junction.

We turn right at the junction and follow the roadway down the hill. As we reach the heart of the village there's a quoits pitch on the right and the Board Inn on the left hand side and, after crossing the roadbridge, we turn right to return to our starting point in the car park.

WALKS FOR ALL SEASONS **AUTUMN: Walk 5**

Sunderland Bridge & Tudhoe

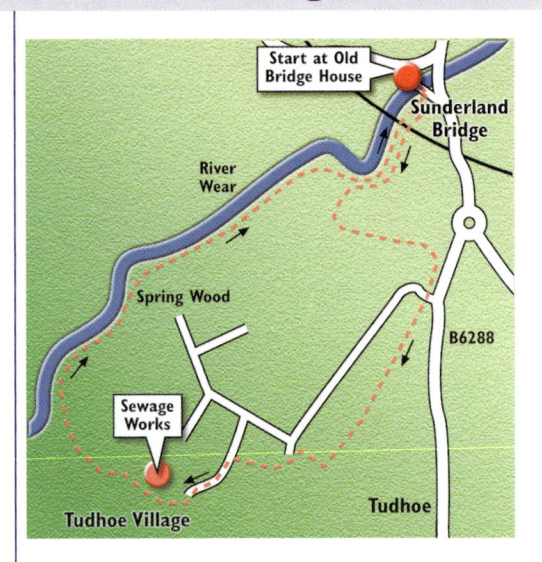

Walk Facts

COUNTY DURHAM

Exploring the bridges of the Wear

START: Old Bridge House, Sunderland Bridge (two miles south of Durham City, off A167).

DISTANCE: 5 1/4 miles.

GOING: Several moderate gradients.

REFRESHMENTS: Venues in Tudhoe and Spennymoor.

MAP: Ordnance Survey Landranger 93 Middlesbrough-Darlington area.

WALKS FOR ALL SEASONS   **AUTUMN: Walk 5**

SUNDERLAND Bridge - two miles South of Durham City on the A167 - is an ideal starting point for exploring a section of the River Wear to the north of Tudhoe Village.

Starting from Old Bridge House - just off the B6300 at Sunderland Bridge - we cross the old stone bridge with the new bridge carrying the A167 away on the left. After crossing we turn right along the bridleway and head towards the railway viaduct.

As the river bends to the right we head diagonally left between posts into the woodland. Continuing up the slope through the woods, we turn left when the path divides and there are seats along this stretch for those in need of a rest.

The pathway crosses duckboards and at the

Enjoy views of the River Wear

next fork in the route we head to the right - with willow trees on our left and a valley below on the right. Walking through to the houses next to the Daleside Arms on the B6288 we bear right behind the public house to follow the footpath over a wooden footbridge and along the right hand field edge.

After crossing a stile we pass under pylons and after the next stile we turn right through a gap in the hedge before following the left hand edge of the arable field.

Our route runs directly ahead towards houses at the northern end of Tudhoe Green and when we reach the wide open area

WALKS FOR ALL SEASONS　　　　　　**AUTUMN: Walk 5**

of the green, bear right to pass Tudhoe Hall Farm House on the left. At Eden House (no 38) we head left to pass through a gate on the far right hand corner of the grassy area and after crossing a stile into the field we turn right and walk towards the bottom left hand corner of the sloping pasture.

Beyond the stile we follow a gravel path to the right - with a valley on the left and at the roadway we turn left towards the sewage works. Just before the gates we turn left along a trackway that runs beside a metal fence and into the woodland.

Gorse bushes and silver birch trees are prominent as we follow the path downhill and when it divides we turn right to reach a level section between fir trees. The pathway soon reaches the riverbank where we turn right to cross a planked footbridge and after passing a long flight of steps on the right we cross two more planked footbridges.

There's a sheep field on the right as we head towards a junction of paths and at this point we bear left beside the riverbank. Continuing along the level stretch the impressive brickwork of the railway viaduct is prominent in the distance and our path runs directly ahead to pass under the arches and back to our starting point on the far side of the road bridge.

The old stone bridge at Sunderland Bridge

WALKS FOR ALL SEASONS **AUTUMN: Walk 6**

Wass Circular

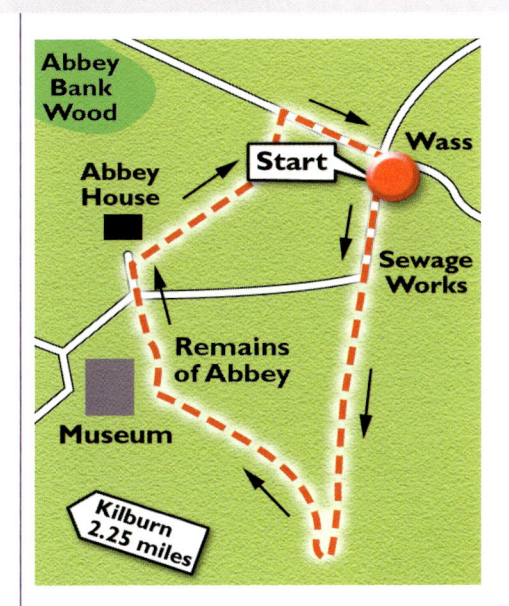

Map labels: Abbey Bank Wood, Abbey House, Wass, Start, Sewage Works, Remains of Abbey, Museum, Kilburn 2.25 miles

NORTH YORK MOORS

Abbey habit on the edge of the National Park

Start: Wombwell Arms, Wass.

Distance: 2¾ miles.

Going: Mainly level.

Refreshments: Wombwell Arms, Wass.

Map: Ordnance Survey Outdoor Leisure 26 North York Moors, Western Area.

WALKS FOR ALL SEASONS   **AUTUMN: Walk 6**

WASS is a delightful little village on the southern fringe of the North York Moors National Park between Kilburn and Ampleforth - and an ideal starting point for a closer look at Byland Abbey.

Starting from the Wombwell Arms at the heart of the village, we walk in a southerly direction down the main road to pass 'Dingley Dell' and a row of estate cottages with the date 1897 on the left.

'The shop' is prominent on the right hand side of the roadway as we continue towards the right hand bend. At the bend we continue directly ahead along the track - with a stone wall close on the left and distant views of Byland Abbey away on the right.

Wass - a delightful village

A hedge lines the next section of track as we head up the slope to pass through a wooden field gate before making our way down the sloping field. At the bottom of the field a wooden post marks the point where we turn right -with a line of hawthorn bushes on the left. Continuing through a gap (with waymarker) we can make out the ruins of Byland Abbey directly ahead.

At the boundary fence we bear right and walk across to a stile in the roadside hedge. The entrance to the abbey is a short distance away on the left.

WALKS FOR ALL SEASONS   **AUTUMN: Walk 6**

In its present ruined state, it is difficult to appreciate that this Cistercian abbey had a church and cloister bigger than Fountains or Rievaulx.

Its main glory is the west front - which has what must have been a magnificent rose window measuring 26ft in diameter.

The ruins of Byland Abbey - it was bigger than Fountains or Rievaulx

From the abbey, we cross the road and walk up the driveway that leads to Abbey House. Just before the gate posts we turn right to pass through a wooden field gate and, at the end of the stone wall, another wooden gate leads into the large sloping field.

We bear left up the rounded slope and make our way across the field to reach a kissing gate in the top left hand corner.

Veering to the left, we soon come to a stile next to the metal field gate. The right of way then runs directly ahead to another wooden field gate. A simple plank bridge crosses the beck and, at the junction with the side lane, we turn right down the gentle slope.

The stony lane soon runs past Woodside on the left and Brook Cottage on the right before reaching Lime Tree Cottage on the corner of the roadway opposite our starting point at the Wombwell Arms.

WALKS FOR ALL SEASONS   **AUTUMN: Walk 6**

A tranquil scene at Bylands Abbey

Walks to banish winter's blues

WINTER walks can be most rewarding, can't they? An invigorating walk during a break in the worst weather of the year works wonders for lifting the spirits - but it is important to take all sensible precautions.

Plenty of warm and waterproof clothing and footwear is an absolute must as are hot drinks while relevant, detailed maps of the proposed route assume prime importance at this time of the year.

Allowing plenty of time to complete the walk during daylight and leaving details of your proposed route with a third party are other sensible precautions to take.

Having said that, the winter landscape has its own unique appeal, with skeletal trees and bushes often enhanced by layers of snow and frost.

With limited daylight hours and potentially tricky underfoot conditions, this batch of walks is focussed closer to local townships, ranging from the coastline at Redcar and Marske to the rolling countryside around Richmond in Swaledale. For the most part, however, these routes cover level stretches of ground with plenty of opportunities to work up a brisk pace and banish any prospect of those winter blues!

WALKS FOR ALL SEASONS *WINTER: Walk 1*

Carlton Miniott & Sandhutton

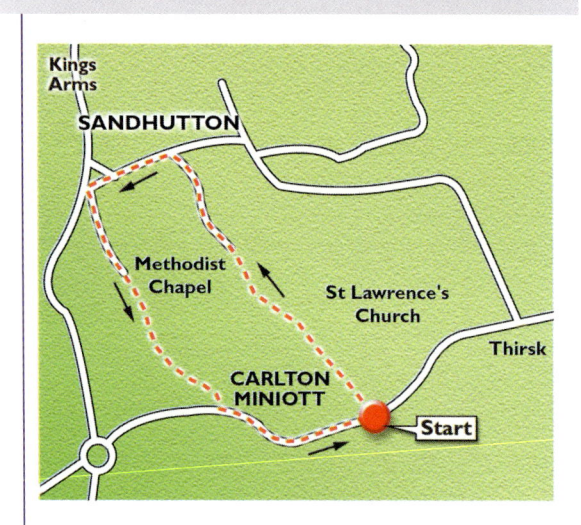

NORTH YORKSHIRE

A rewarding stroll on little-used footpaths

START: Dog And Gun Inn, Carlton Miniott.

DISTANCE: 3 miles.

GOING: Level all the way. Field paths and tracks, but several stiles.

REFRESHMENTS: Dog And Gun, Carlton Miniott; King's Arms, Sandhutton.

MAP: Ordnance Survey Landranger 99. Northallerton and Ripon.

WALKS FOR ALL SEASONS **WINTER: Walk 1**

IT'S really rewarding to discover little-used footpaths in pleasant country areas - with half hidden stiles, gates and way markers along the way.

You can do just that while enjoying a stroll between the villages of Carlton Miniott and Sandhutton - close to the A61 on the west side of Thirsk.

Starting from the Dog And Gun at the centre of Carlton Miniott, we cross the road with care and make our way through the left hand side of St Lawrence's churchyard to reach a boundary hedge.

Continuing through a gap next to the field gate, we walk directly ahead along the left hand field edge and then follow the clear route across the middle of the next field.

The Hambleton Hills form a distant backcloth away on the right but our stretch is level and, after cross-

In a hedgerow - the village pump at Carlton Miniott

WALKS FOR ALL SEASONS　　　　　WINTER: Walk 1

ing a stile in the wooden fence, we continue directly ahead - with a hedgerow close on our right. As the field edge begins to bear left, we make our way through the strip of bracken to reach another stile in the fence.

We follow the left hand field edge straight ahead until it bends into a wide track on the left hand side. This level section soon veers left to run between high hedges and out to the public roadway.

Turning left along the road, we soon pass the Old Vicarage on the left and St Mary's church on high ground close to the left hand verge.

Church House and Church Farm are prominent on the right as we reach the broad green and, as we continue around the left hand edge of the green, Ivy House (1896), Porch House and Home Garth come into view.

The Methodist Chapel of 1815 forms a contrast with the houses and we pass Wesley Cottage on the left before the west side of the green joins the A167. The King's Arms is on the opposite corner as we bear left along the main road and then immediately follow a track away to the left between hedges.

After crossing a stile next to a metal field gate, we continue directly ahead on a grassy strip between large fields. The Hambleton Hills line the left hand horizon and far away to the right we can make out high ground beyond Leyburn and Wensleydale in the west.

After crossing a stile in the hedgerow, we walk directly ahead and properties at Carlton Miniott come into view away on the left. At the strip of woodland we turn right to follow the field edge round into the layby.

Continuing round to the left, we make our way along the

WALKS FOR ALL SEASONS WINTER: Walk 1

roadside verge into Carlton Miniott with Durham Ox Cottage on the left and Manor Farm on the right.

Crossing the A61 with care, it's surprising what you can pick out on this busy route - starting with the village pump in the hedgerow on the right hand side.

Our starting point at the village inn is a little further along the roadway.

St Mary's Church at Sandhutton

Maltby Circular

TEESSIDE

Historical paths start at the Pathfinders

START: The Pathfinders, Maltby village.
DISTANCE: 2¾ miles.
GOING: Fairly level for much of route. Slopes close to Thornton and steep hill on road back into Maltby.
REFRESHMENTS: Pathfinders, Maltby village.
MAP: Ordnance Survey Outdoor Leisure 26 North York Moors Western Area.

WALKS FOR ALL SEASONS — WINTER: Walk 2

THE quiet village of Maltby has a long history stretching back into the Middle Ages - with the local hostelry serving as a reminder of more recent times at nearby Thornaby aerodrome.

Starting from the Pathfinders pub, we walk in a westerly direction through the village before turning left at the Methodist Chapel into Roger Lane.

We soon pass Westlands on the left and continue along the tree-lined roadway towards Hilton - with the buildings of Maltby Farm on the left-hand side. The road rises gently and we then pass the cluster of brick buildings at Maltby Grange on the right.

As the roadway bends sharply to the right, we turn left to cross a stile next to the metal field gate and follow the wide track directly ahead. At the first right-hand turn in the track, we turn left over a step-through stile into the field and then walk directly ahead towards the fence.

Turning right before the fence, we follow the field edge beside the beck (on our left). After about 70 yards, we cross the wooden footbridge over the beck and turn right to make our way to the corner of the field. A stile next to the metal field gate leads into another field and we follow the right-hand edge along a very muddy but level stretch.

A step-through stile leads to a wide trackway and, after crossing, we continue over another stile and along the right-hand edge of the field. There's yet another stile next to a set of metal gates as we make our way directly ahead and we can soon see the cluster of buildings at Thornton Grange on the right-hand side. Continuing down the right-hand field edge - with a newly-planted hedgerow close at hand - we turn right at the bottom of the field.

After about 40 yards we turn left through a gap in the hedgerow at the top of the slope above Maltby Beck.

Bearing left at this point, we make our way down the slope to cross the wooden footbridge and then continue up the sloping field towards a metal field gate. We turn left before the gate and walk along the top edge of the field to cross a wooden stile next to the metal field gate.

There are two more stiles as we continue above Maltby Beck in a north-westerly direction and then make our way down a grassy slope towards a stile beside Maltby Road. Turning left along the roadway, we soon pass Throstle Nest on the left and it's important to face oncoming traffic as we follow the bend round to the right and then up the hill.

At the top of the hill we pass Maltby House on the corner of Willows Avenue and continue along High Lane past the village store and White House (on the right) - with Irishannon on the left - as we return to our starting point.

The Pathfinders at Maltby

WALKS FOR ALL SEASONS   **WINTER: Walk 3**

Nunthorpe Station & Ormesby

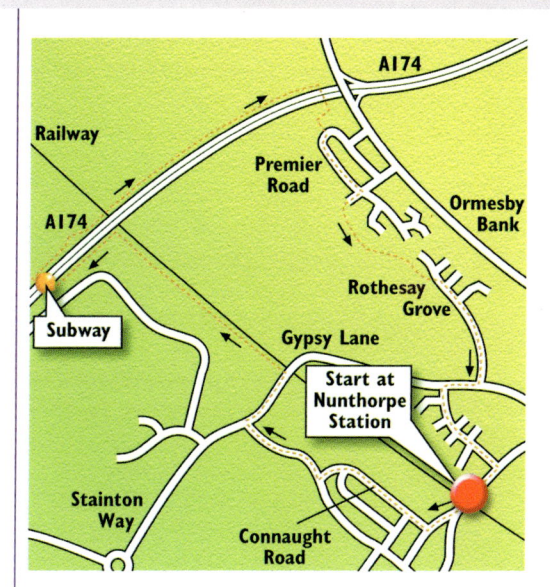

TEESSIDE

Rewards of meeting an urban challenge

START: Nunthorpe Station.

DISTANCE: 3½ miles.

GOING: Moderate/ severe gradient on return section.

REFRESHMENTS: Venues in Marton and Nunthorpe.

MAP: Middlesbrough A-Z, pages 92-93 and 76-77.

WALKS FOR ALL SEASONS   WINTER: Walk 3

IT IS a real challenge to find pleasant footpaths among Middlesbrough's southern suburbs and, as a reward, there are some interesting surprises along the way.

Starting from Nunthorpe Station we walk in a westerly direction along Marton Moor Road before turning right at Nunthorpe Methodist Church into Connaught Road. The roadway soon slopes downhill and a left hand bend at the bottom of the hill leads to the junction with The Avenue.

We turn right along the Avenue and, after passing shops on the right, the roadway rises before sloping down to the junction with Gypsy Lane where we turn right and soon pass High Gill on the right. Just before the railway we bear left to follow the footpath along the field edge and round to the left before running down a flight of wooden steps and across a metal footbridge.

The pathway then runs beside Cypress Road before turning right to pass under the A174 Parkway. As the tarmac path bears left, we turn right up the grassy slope - with Ormesby Beck and the A174 on our right. The pathway soon veers to the right across a concrete bridge and then veers to the left to pass under a stone-built railway bridge.

Keeping to the right of farm buildings at Ormesby Grange, we pass through a kissing gate close to the fence and make our way down another flight of steps and along the field edge - with views of Eston Nab and Ormesby Church directly ahead.

After passing through a field gate, we have a fine view of Ormesby Hall on the left. As we reach the churchyard, our route runs round to the left to the lychgate. We turn right along Church Lane and, at the top of the roadway, we follow the footpath on the left and across the footbridge over the A174 Parkway.

WALKS FOR ALL SEASONS　　　　　　　**WINTER: Walk 3**

On the far side of the bridge, we turn right and then left into Meadow Close where a lane runs directly ahead between privet hedges into Premier Road. Following the roadway round to the right, it soon veers left up the hill and at the junction we turn right into Spring Gardens Lane.

A lane leads into Crow Wood, which is managed by the Tees Valley Wildlife Trust. Walkers are requested to follow the countryside code on the route through the woodland as it runs to the left and up the slope.

Ormesby Churchyard

As the strip of woodland narrows, our pathway bears left into Rothesay Grove where we turn right to make our way up the hill and round the right hand bend to reach the junction with Gypsy Lane.

Turning right, we soon pass Beadlam Avenue (on the left) and then turn left into Beverley Road. We continue directly ahead along Beverley Road to the junction with Guisborough Road, with views of Roseberry Topping ahead, where we turn right to make our way back to our starting point at Nunthorpe Station.

WALKS FOR ALL SEASONS **WINTER: Walk 3**

A wintery Roseberry Topping, from near Nunthorpe

WALKS FOR ALL SEASONS **WINTER: Walk 4**

Redcar & Marske

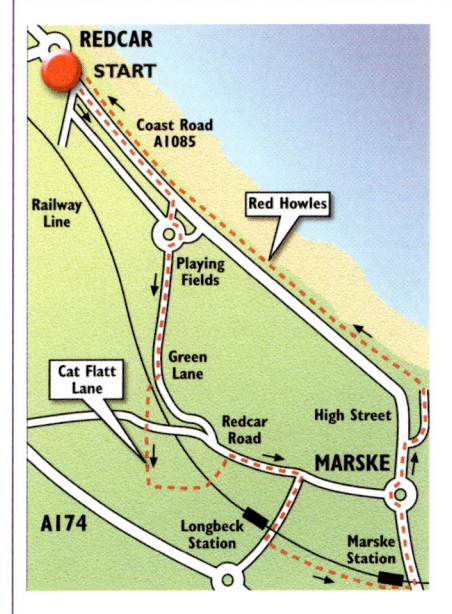

Cleveland coast

A bracing stroll along the shoreline

START: Roundabout at northern end of coast road (A1085).

DISTANCE: 3¾ miles.

GOING: Level.

REFRESHMENTS: Venues in Redcar and Marske.

MAP: Middlesbrough A-Z, pages 28-29 and 44-45.

WALKS FOR ALL SEASONS　　　　　　WINTER: Walk 4

WHEN our winter weather rules out walking in the countryside, then it's time for a bracing stroll along a section of our splendid local coastline.

Starting from the roundabout at the northern end of Redcar Coast Road (A1085) we walk along the Stray past Zetland Park on the right and roadside houses before turning right into Green Lane.

Continuing directly ahead at the roundabout, we pass a playing field on the left and Mackinlay Park (home of Redcar RFC) covers ground on the right. The firm pathway then runs between lines of bushes on both sides to reach the Middlesbrough to Saltburn railway line and, after crossing with care, we turn left to follow the gravel track directly ahead towards Redcar Road.

Just before the public road, the track veers to the right and great care is needed when crossing this busy roadway. A footpath sign directs us away from the road along Cat Flatt Lane - with views of New Marske and Errington Woods directly ahead.

When this wide grassy track splits, we bear left and soon see houses close to Cat Flatt crossing. Continuing across the rail track, we follow Cat Flatt Lane to the junction with Redcar Road and then bear right towards the centre of Marske.

Opposite the Mermaid public house, we bear right into Longbeck Road and continue over the railway track before turning immediately to the left along the 'Black Path' that runs beside the tracks. In fact, it's a pleasant enough path - with some fine views across open land along the way - and Marske railway station soon comes into view. The track continues past the station and down the slope to reach the A1085 road.

It's not easy to spot the older properties among modern shop frontages and business premises but the former Methodist

Chapel is prominent on the left as we head down the High Street towards the roundabout. On the other side of the roundabout, No 162 High Street is a fine example of a cruck house and is said to date from around 1500AD.

Continuing along the main street, we reach the Ship Inn and, as we follow the roadway round to the right, look out for the stone-built former police house on the left. The High Street soon veers to the left and runs downhill - with Valley Gardens on the right and some interesting old cottages along Cliff Terrace on the left.

Cliff House - originally the holiday residence of Joseph Pease - covers nearby high ground as we walk down the slipway and then bear left along the sands. From here you can usually see several vessels lying offshore waiting to enter Tees Bay.

Continuing along the sands, we pass the narrow inlets of Flat Howle, Scanbeck Howle and Bydale Howle. Redcar and Coatham landmarks soon come into view and at either Red Howles or Millclose Howle we make our way from the beach to higher ground. Turning right, we walk along the grassy expanse of the Stray to return to our starting point at the northern end of the Coast Road.

The view along Redcar Stray to Cliff House

WALKS FOR ALL SEASONS   **WINTER: Walk 5**

Richmond & Skeeby

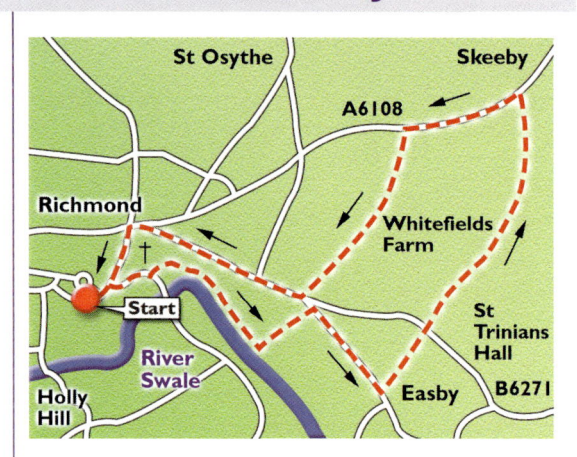

NORTH YORKSHIRE

Town and country: the best of both worlds

START: Centre of Richmond market place.

DISTANCE: 4 1/2 miles.

GOING: Mainly firm pathways with some field walking and few moderate gradients.

REFRESHMENTS: Many venues in Richmond.

MAP: Ordnance Survey, Landranger 92, Barnard Castle.

WALKS FOR ALL SEASONS   **WINTER: Walk 5**

THE CENTRE of Richmond has so many places of interest that it's easy to overlook some scenic routes through nearby countryside.

Why not get the best of both worlds by combining a look at some of the town's fine buildings with a stroll through gently rolling countryside?

Starting from the centre of the market place, we walk down the north side past the Castle Tavern before turning left into Frenchgate. The impressive frontage of Swale House is on the corner as we bear right into Station Road and we soon pass St Mary's parish church on the slope away to our left.

At the bottom of the hill we turn left into Lombards Wynd and turn right at Acomb House to follow the lane towards Easby Abbey. Passing the Drummer Boy's Stone, we keep to the right

Fine buildings line Richmond's market place

WALKS FOR ALL SEASONS **WINTER: Walk 5**

of the field and follow the metal fence along the riverside path. At the start of the wooden fence, we turn left into the field and follow the track up the slope to reach the roadway.

Turning right along the metalled roadway towards Easby, we make our way down the slope towards a terrace of cottages which were set up as a hospital by William Smith, Rector of

The Castle Tavern in Richmond market place

Melsonby, in 1752. Just before the cottages we turn left and soon pass Easby Mews on the right as we continue directly ahead through a field gate and up a sloping field.

The right of way runs between stone walls on both sides before running down a slope to a metal field gate beside the roadway. After crossing with care, we follow the concrete track that leads towards St Trinian's and at the open area our route continues to the right along the gravel trackway.

The right of way soon joins Stony Close and as the track bends to the right we walk directly ahead on a level, grassy stretch. There are two metal field gates along the next section before we cross a cattle grid close to the A6108.

Turning left along the public road we follow the footpath on the right towards Richmond and just before the strip of woodland on the right we come across a row of four houses including Thornlea. We turn left after this short terrace along a concrete track that bends through an area of woodland.

The path may be extremely muddy in places but becomes firmer as we reach open countryside with a wire fence on our right-hand side and follow the route directly ahead to join a wide track that runs past Garden Cottage and down the slope to reach the B6271.

We turn right along the raised pavement of Maison Dieu and as the roadway veers gently to the left there are fine views across Richmond.

Continuing round to the left, we join Darlington Road and at the war memorial turn left down the sloping roadway of Frenchgate. There are some fine frontages on buildings as we continue down Frenchgate towards Swale House before retracing our steps back up the slope to return to our starting point in the market place.

WALKS FOR ALL SEASONS   *WINTER: Walk 6*

Stokesley & Broughton Bridge

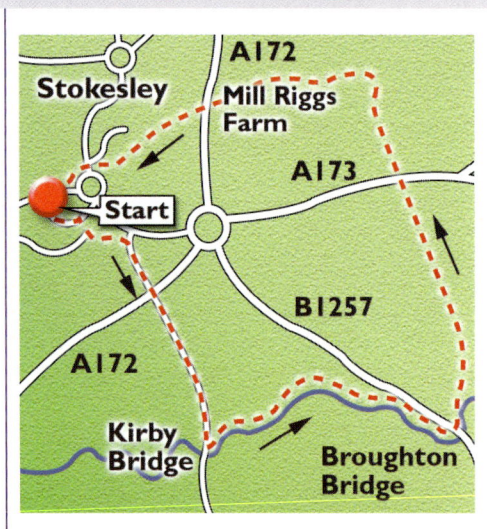

Walk Facts

NORTH YORKSHIRE

Taking a country walk to the shops

START: Town Hall on Stokesley High Street.

DISTANCE: 3 miles.

GOING: Level.

REFRESHMENTS: Venues in Stokesley.

MAP: Ordnance Survey Outdoor Leisure 26, North York Moors Western Area.

WALKS FOR ALL SEASONS　　　　　　**WINTER: Walk 6**

STOKESLEY is one of those places where it's easy to combine a spot of shopping and sightseeing with a gentle stroll through level countryside close to the township.

Starting from the Town Hall (built 1854) at the eastern end of the High Street, we walk along the south side of the market place towards the manor house.

At the end of the properties we turn right and follow the pathway through the churchyard with the church of St Peter and St Paul prominent on the right.

The path leads through to the River Leven and, after crossing the white-painted footbridge, we bear left (with a stone wall on the right).

Our walk around Stokesley starts at the Town Hall (above) and takes us through the Churchyard (left)

At the public road we turn right and soon pass Leven Bridge House before making our way into Station Road. The buildings of Stokesley School are on our left as we continue past Hambleton Court (on the right) and just beyond the large glass houses we reach Kirby Bridge.

Immediately after the bridge we turn left along the beckside path and soon reach a wooden field gate and stile before a roadway.

After crossing with care, we continue directly ahead along the grassy verge - with fine views of the Cleveland Hills away on the right. Close to the junction of becks we cross a wooden footbridge and walk ahead to reach a stile next to Broughton Bridge.

Turning left, we cross the bridge then cross the B1257 road with care and follow the pathway that soon veers round to the left to reach the A173 Stokesley to Great Ayton road.

Again care is needed as we cross to walk directly ahead beside the water course (on our right). As the main channel bears right, we turn left to cross a wooden stile in the fence and then follow the path beside an arable field on the right and the river below on the left.

The path leads through to a metal field gate next to the A172. After crossing with care, a footpath sign directs us ahead - with houses close at hand on the right. We soon reach the Safeway car park and walk along the left hand edge to reach the roadway close to the roundabout.

It's worth taking a look at the water wheel from Stokesley Mill which is on the left close to the bridge and the old animal pound, opposite the New Inn on the right, before heading back into the High Street where our starting point at the Town Hall lies directly ahead.

WALKS FOR ALL SEASONS **WINTER: Walk 6**

The Parish Church of St Peter and St Paul, Stokesley

Notes